Love Poems for Mary

Love Poems for Mary

STEPHEN PEREZ

ISBN: 978-1-971940-60-1 (sc)
ISBN: 978-1-971940-61-8 (e)

Rev. date: 04/01/2026

Contents

Owner of My Heart

Owner of My Heart

by Stephen Perez

You are the owner of my heart
you own me, heart and soul.
I was lonely and dead inside
with no true emotions to show.
Then you came into my life
and you filled the empty hole.
You put a spark back in my heart
filled with love and so much more.
You showed me I could love again
and that life can truly be sweet.
My love for you is strong and true,
and it grows with each passing week.
You told me that you don't want anything serious
and my love might all be in vain,
but I will love you anyway,
and gladly take the pain.
The pain will be hard and it will be deep,
but the memories I have made
will still be just as sweet.
He brought you into my life
and for that I thank God every day,

so if it is his will
in my life is where you will stay.
If things don't work out
and we still have to part,
please just know one thing —
you are the owner of my heart.

A Christmas Wish

A Christmas Wish

By Stephen Perez

Christmas is my favorite time of year.
It's when people are friendlier,
warmer, and more caring.
It's when children of all ages get their wishes granted,
a time when parents can count their blessings.
A Christmas wish is a special one,
a wish that is blessed from above.
My wish this Christmas season
is that you open your heart and capture all my love.
It's a magical time of year
when dreams can and do come true,
a time to make special memories
of loving moments spent with you.
Relationships are special this time of year.
Somehow they seem to flourish.
All of this can happen
with one little Christmas wish.

This Person

This Person

by Stephen Perez

This person, this amazing person
that always drives me crazy,
this person that doesn't know she is beautiful,
she never ceases to amaze me.
This person that never tells me that she loves me,
somehow always lets me know.
She really does love and care for me,
but never lets it show.
This person that holds my heart in her hands,
she means the world to me.
If only she would let me into her life,
how happy I would be.
This person that turns my world upside down,
and if she only knew
how much I really need her,
this amazing person is you.

Our First Kiss

Our First Kiss

by Steven Perez

The first time we kissed was magic.
I didn't want the moment to end.
My head was all a-flutter.
The whole night went by like a whirlwind.
Each time we kiss, I fall deeper,
and I hope I never come out.
My feelings for you grow stronger,
to the whole world I want to shout.
My life would be so much brighter
if only you would open your heart,
give my love a little chance.
That would be such a great start.
Let's get our life started together.
Time is slipping away.
If you would only let me love you,
that would really make my whole day.

A Day Without You

A Day Without You

by Steven Perez

A day without you is like a day without air.
I love everything about you, from
your toes to your hair.
I can't imagine an hour without you,
much less a whole day.
That's like having a pain
that won't go away.
I love you, I need you,
of that there is no doubt.
With your love and your caring,
I can't do without.
I wait till the day
that you wake in my arms,
a day of renewed love,
a life in my heart.

How Do I Love Thee

How Do I Love Thee

By Stephen Perez

I love it when you lean over the
counter to check your phone.
I love it when you wrinkle your nose
when you say certain things.
I love the view when you're walking toward me.
I love the view when you're walking away.
I love the different way you wear your hair.
I love the way you move when you walk.
I love the way you wave when you say goodbye.
I love the way you make me feel when I'm with you.
I definitely love your hugs and kisses.
These are just a few little things I love about you.
Mi vida eres tú, te amo y te canto desde mi corazón.

Translation: "You are my life and I
love you with all my heart."

My Promise

by Steven Perez

I promise I will never hurt you and
I will never make you cry.
I promise to never make you doubt my
love and to never make you ask why.
I promise that I will love you forever and work
to make all of your dreams come true.
I promise to keep you in mind in everything I do.
I promise that you are my only
one and I will never stray.
There is no one else I could ever love quite this way.
I promise that I will take care of you
and never take you for granted.
I can promise all of this because you're
everything I've ever wanted.

On the Wings of Your Love

On the Wings of Your Love

by Stephen Perez

Riding on the wings of your love, I

start to face another day.

With your love in my heart, there is nothing I can't face.

The world can be a scary place, with so much going on.

I just get lost in you, and all my worries are gone.

When I'm with you, you're the only one I see.

There is no place I would rather be.

You make my life complete, you are my world.

You are my everything, without you, I would be lost.

Happiness

Happiness

by Steven Perez

Happiness is being with the one you love and
spending time together, never wanting the
moment to end, to be with you forever.

Happiness is seeing your smiling face every
day and making special memories.

It goes a long way to brighten my day
and it makes me very happy.

Happiness is wanting to spend our days
together, being side by side.

From now until forever, happiness is waiting to
hold and love you, never wanting to part.

You're always on my mind, you're always in my heart.

When It Comes to You

When It Comes to You

by Steven Perez

When it comes to you, I am the biggest fool in town.
Like a little puppy, I follow you all around.
When it comes to you, my love will never die.
You're like a drug to me, and you always keep me high.
When it comes to you, my feelings all go crazy.
I can't even think straight. Everything goes hazy.
I'll be there to share with you all you say and do.
I'll be there always when it comes to you.

I Need You

I Need You

by Stephen Perez

I need you like the flowers need rain.
You're like a breath of fresh air.
You brighten my day.
You make my heart aware.
I need you like romance needs the moon.
You're everything to me.
Time stands still when I'm with you.
There is no one whom I would rather be.
I need you like I need air to breathe.
I can't see my life without you.
You're all I ever think about.
You're there in everything I do.
I need you in my life like a kite needs the wind.
I will always love you from now until the end.

My Senses

My Senses

by Stephen Perez

You make my senses come alive.
You wake them up, all five.
I love to watch you as you move, here and there.
To me, there is no other sight that can compare.
I love to listen to the sound of your voice.
Whenever I hear it, it makes me rejoice.
I love the taste of your lips.
They bring me joy.
They make me realize that I am a very lucky boy.
I love the smell of your hair as I lean in to kiss you.
It smells like flowers and the morning dew.
I love the feel of your skin next to mine.
It's as intoxicating as a glass of wine.